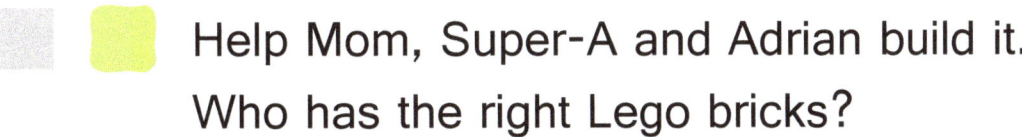

Help Mom, Super-A and Adrian build it.
Who has the right Lego bricks?

 Adrian and Super-A want to bake.
How much coconut do they need? And sugar?

 Help Super-A to tidy up.
Where does everything go?

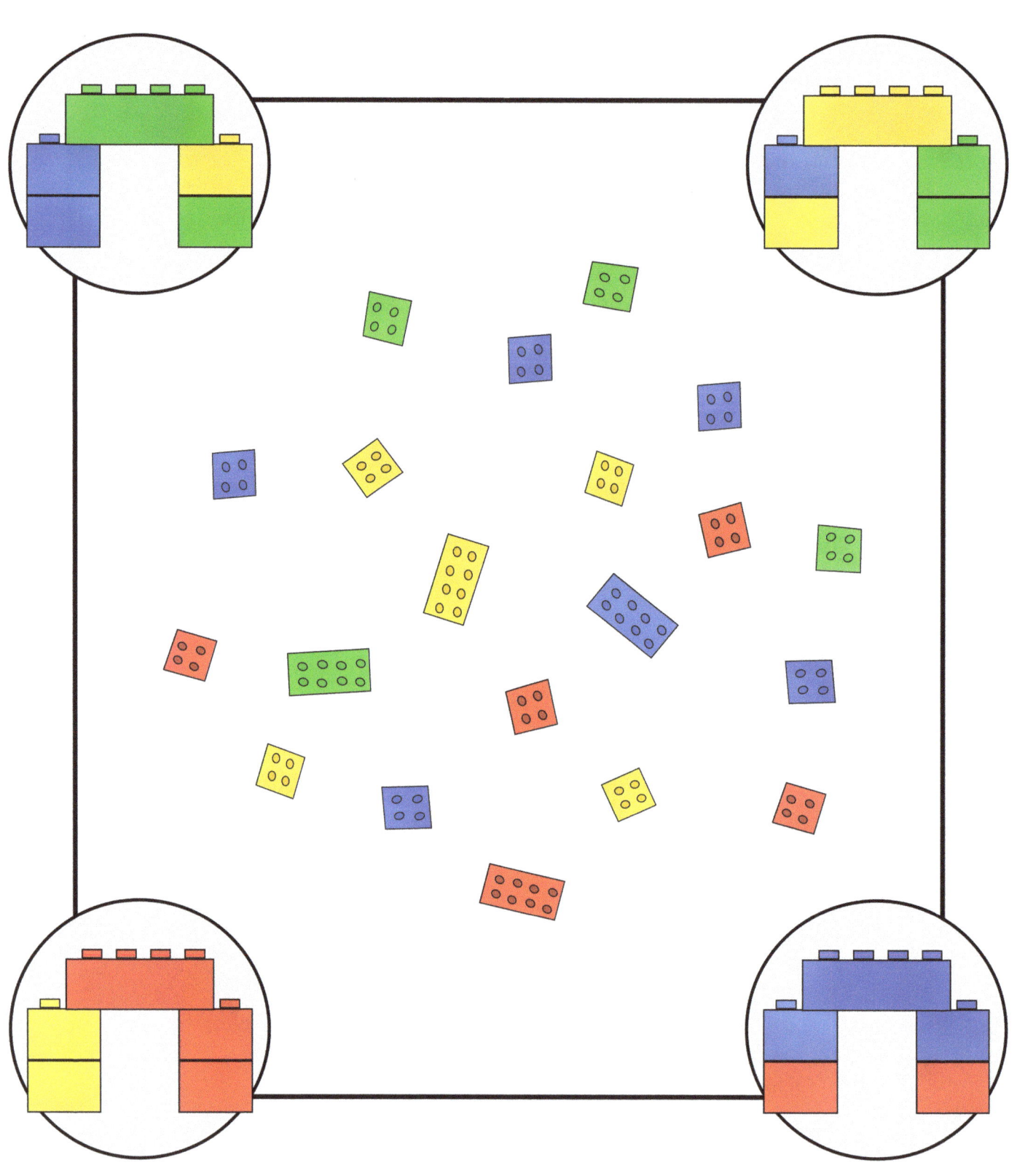

Divide **ALL** Bricks

It is cookie time! Help Adrian sort things on the table. What do you use to wash hands, draw or eat cookies?

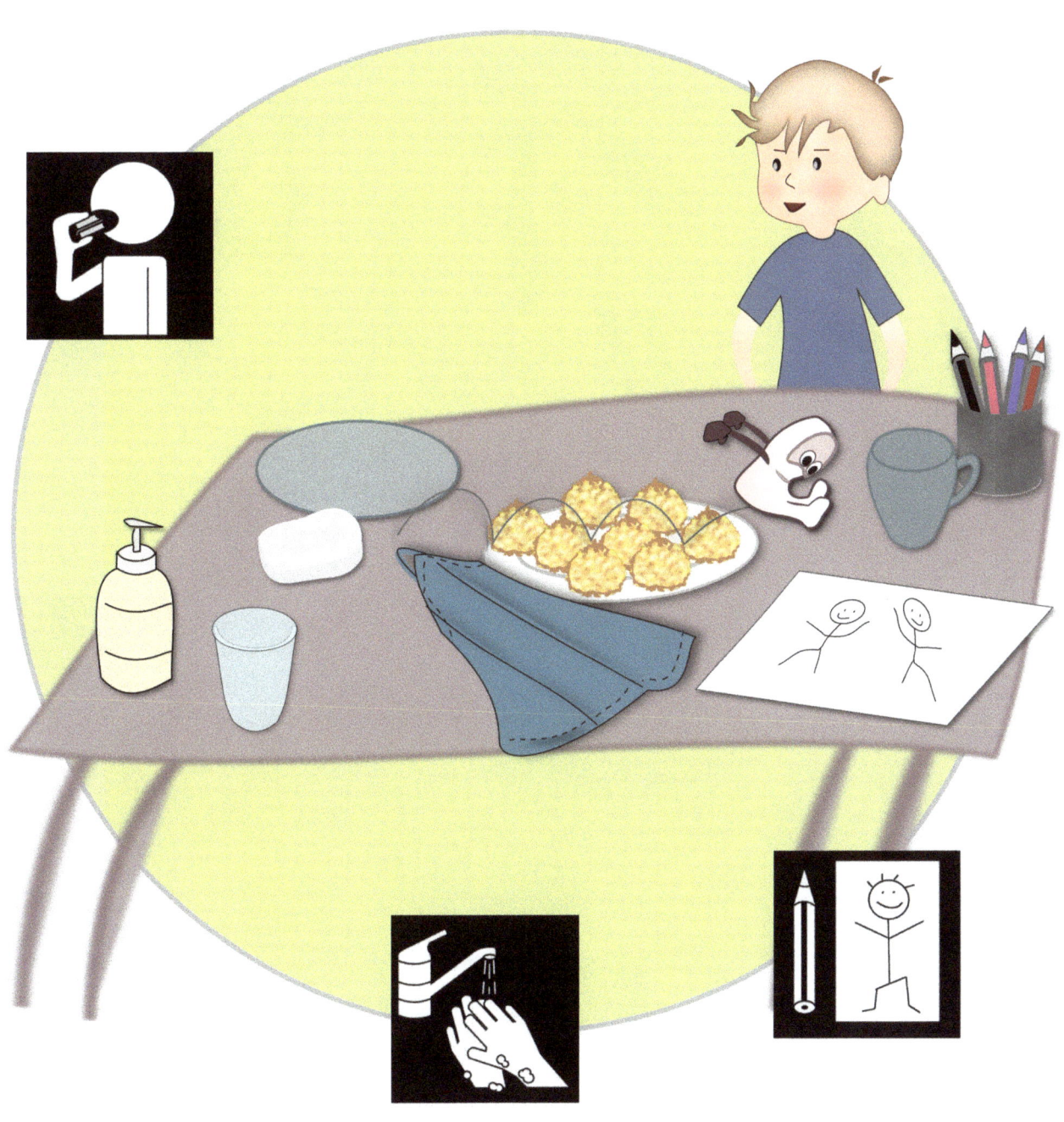

Super-A wants to play! Help Super-A sort it all. What do you use to bake, eat cookies or play?

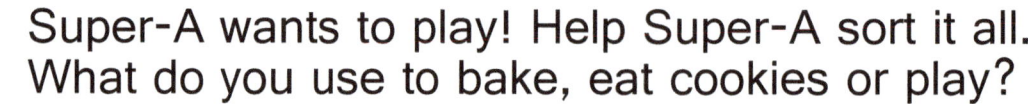

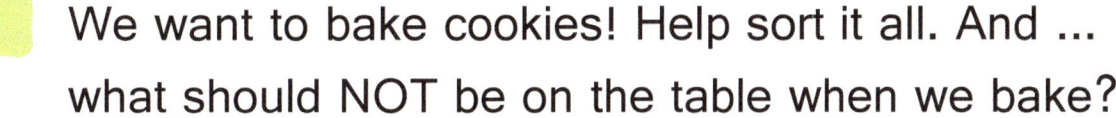

We want to bake cookies! Help sort it all. And ... what should NOT be on the table when we bake?

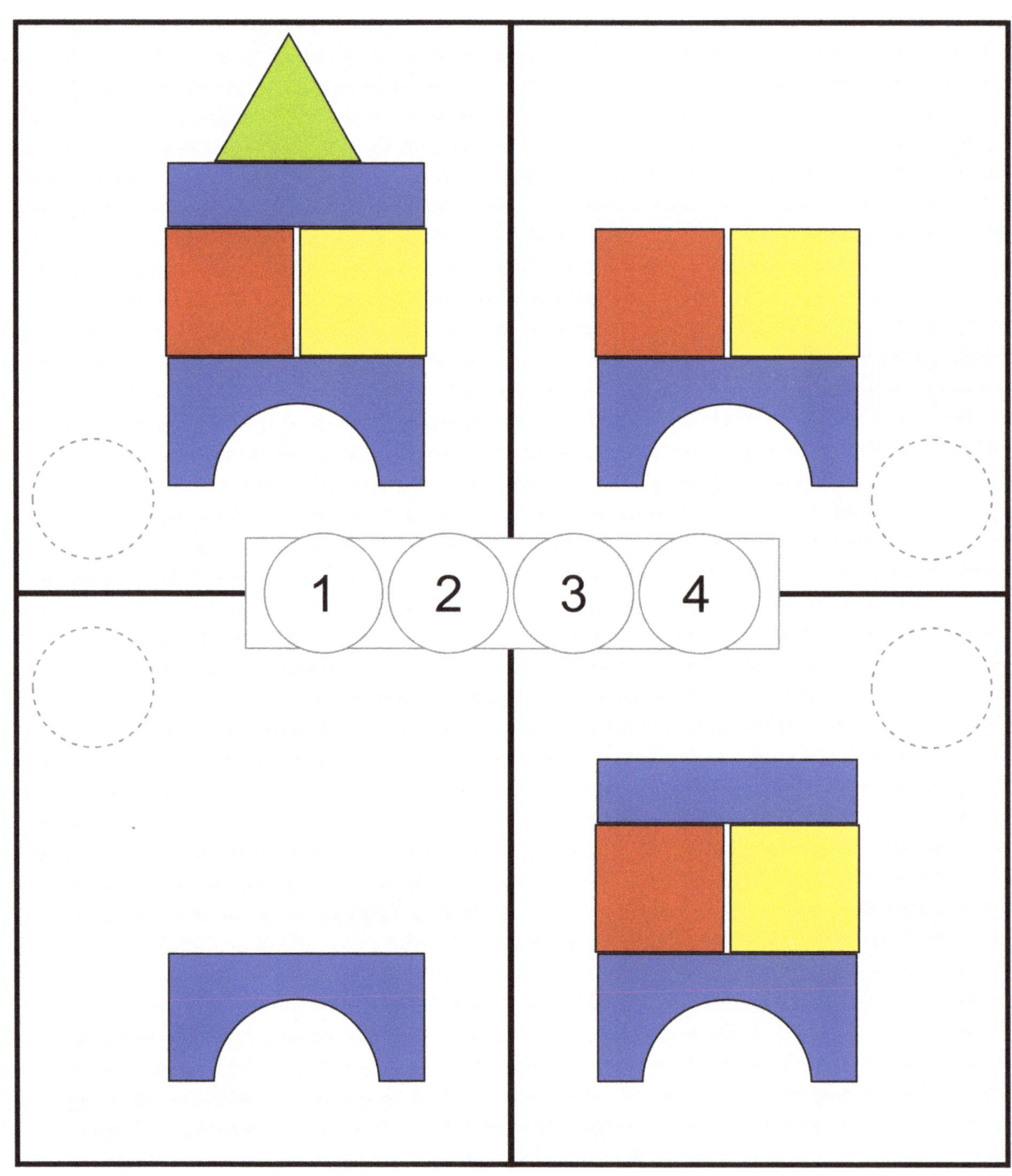

Find **RIGHT** Order

(Write, draw a line or use the cut-outs from the final pages.)

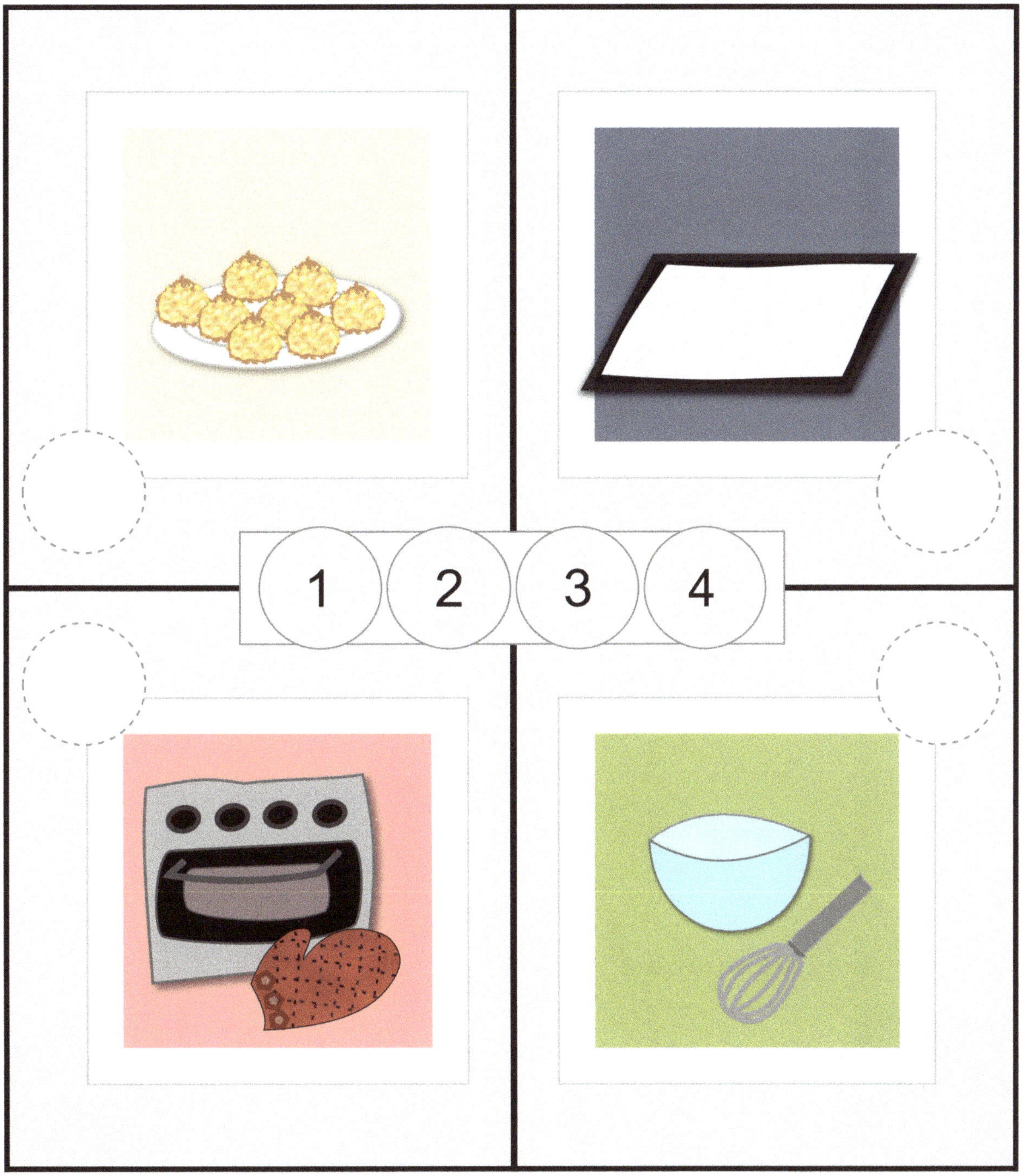

 Adrian and Super-A want to bake cookies. Help them!
In what order do they need the plate and the other things?

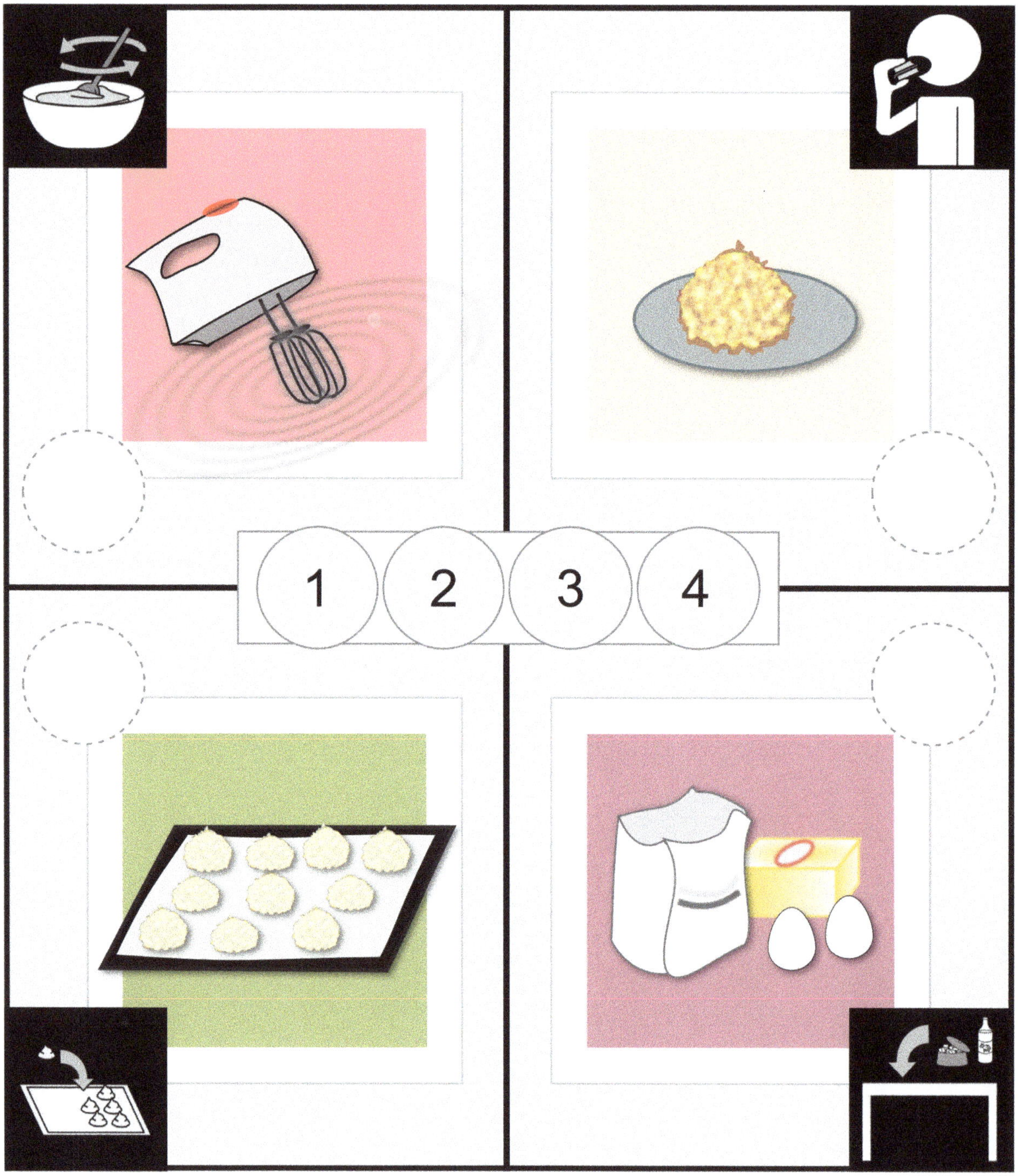

How do you bake cookies?
Help Adrian and Super-A to do things in the right order!

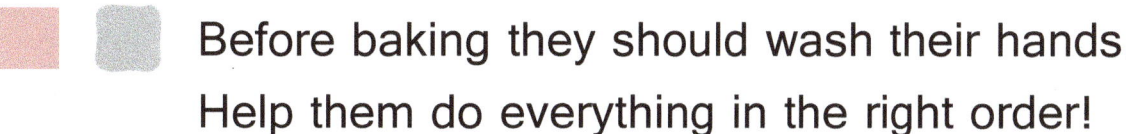
Before baking they should wash their hands.
Help them do everything in the right order!

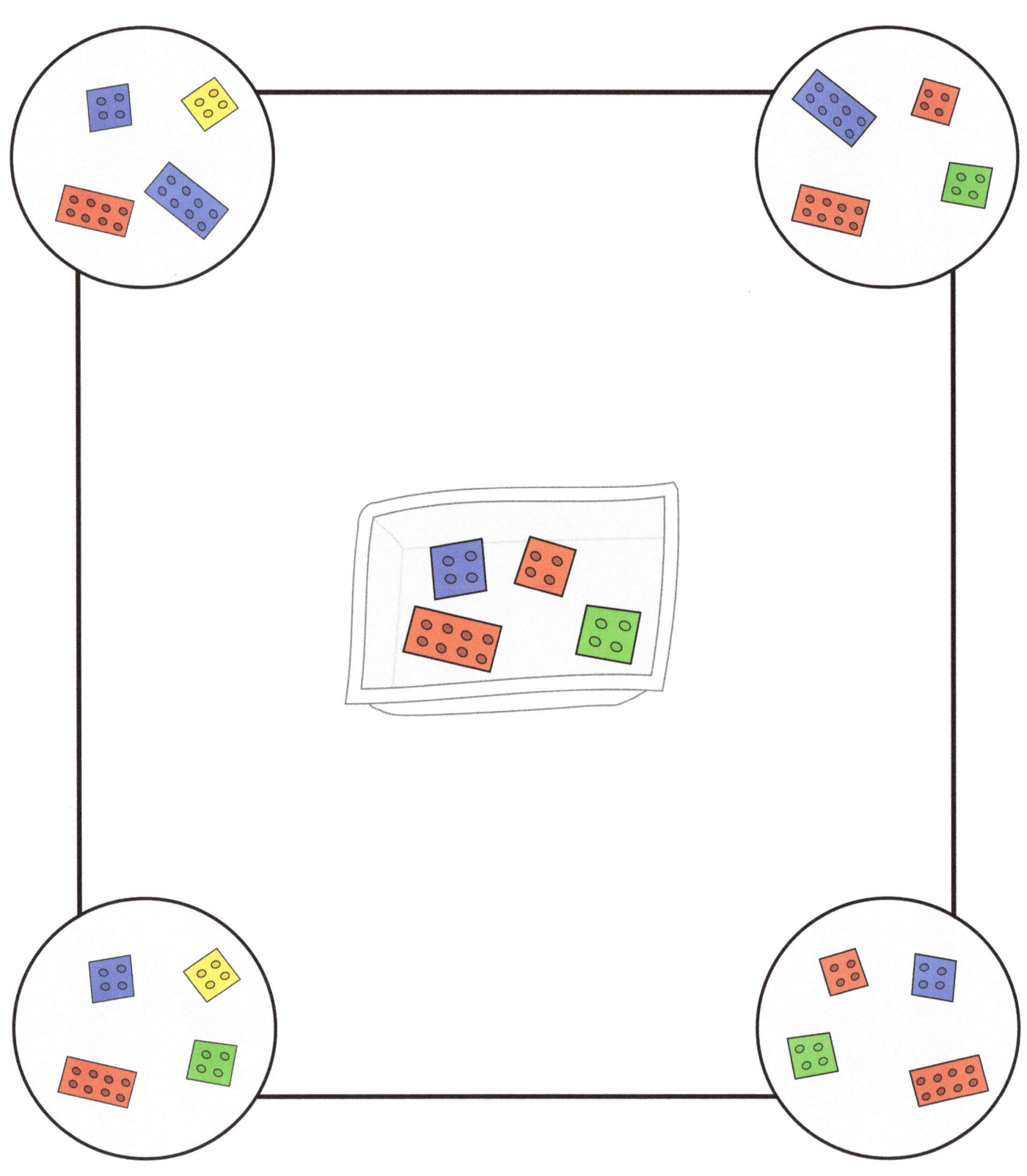

Find **4** Same

Everybody is thirsty. Give them something they like to drink.
(Give each person one green cut-out from the final pages.)

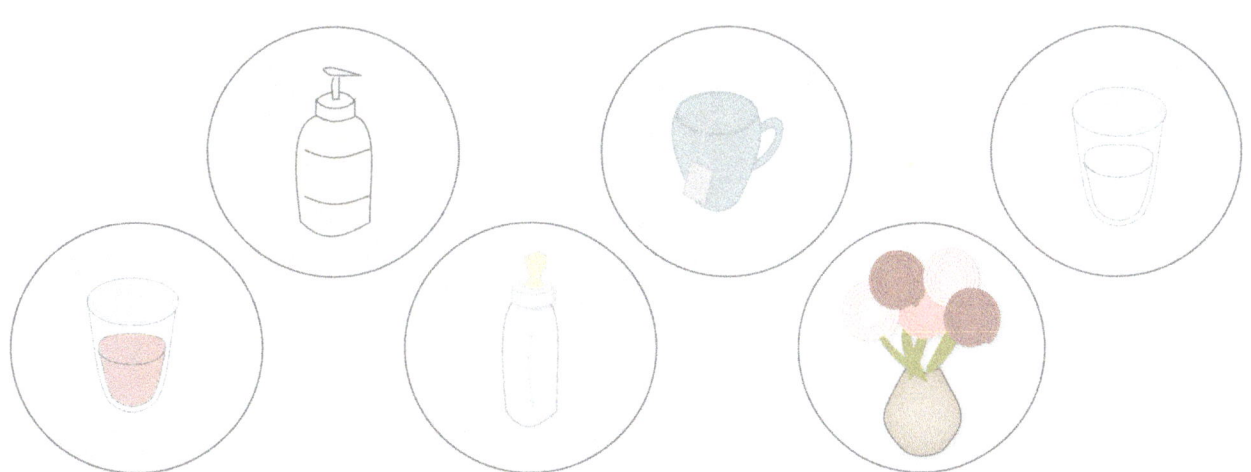

Everybody wants to go outside.
Help them find something they would like to put on.

Super-A, Adrian and their Little Brother want to play. There are 6 toys. Give 1 toy to each of them.

Find SAME Rows

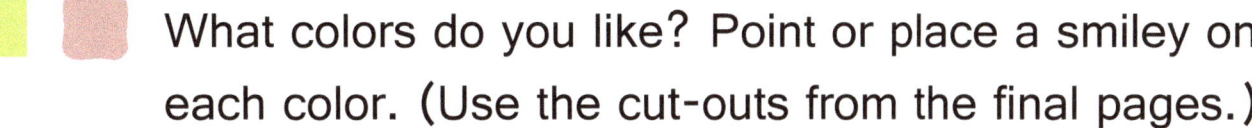 What colors do you like? Point or place a smiley on each color. (Use the cut-outs from the final pages.)

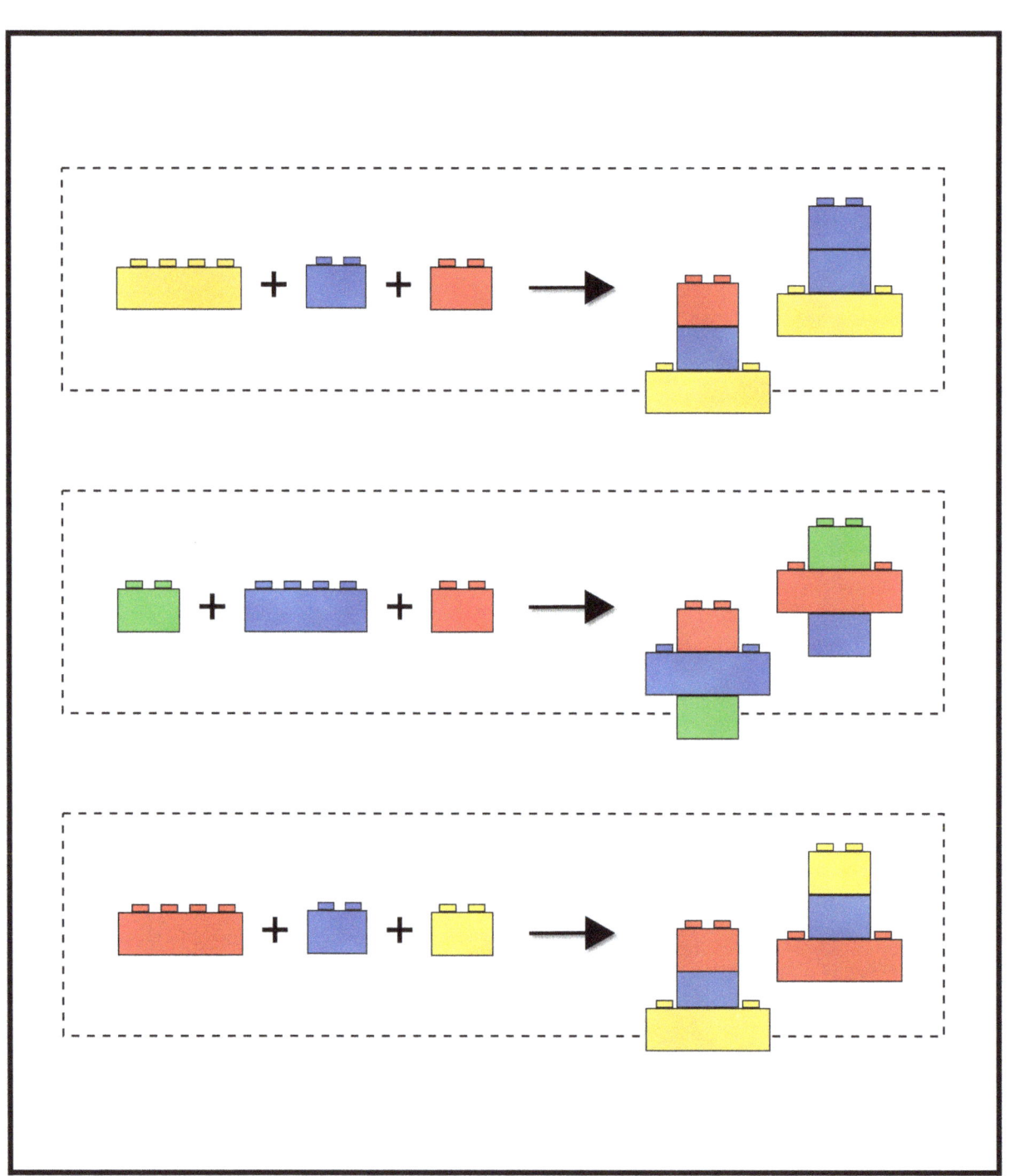

Find RIGHT Solution

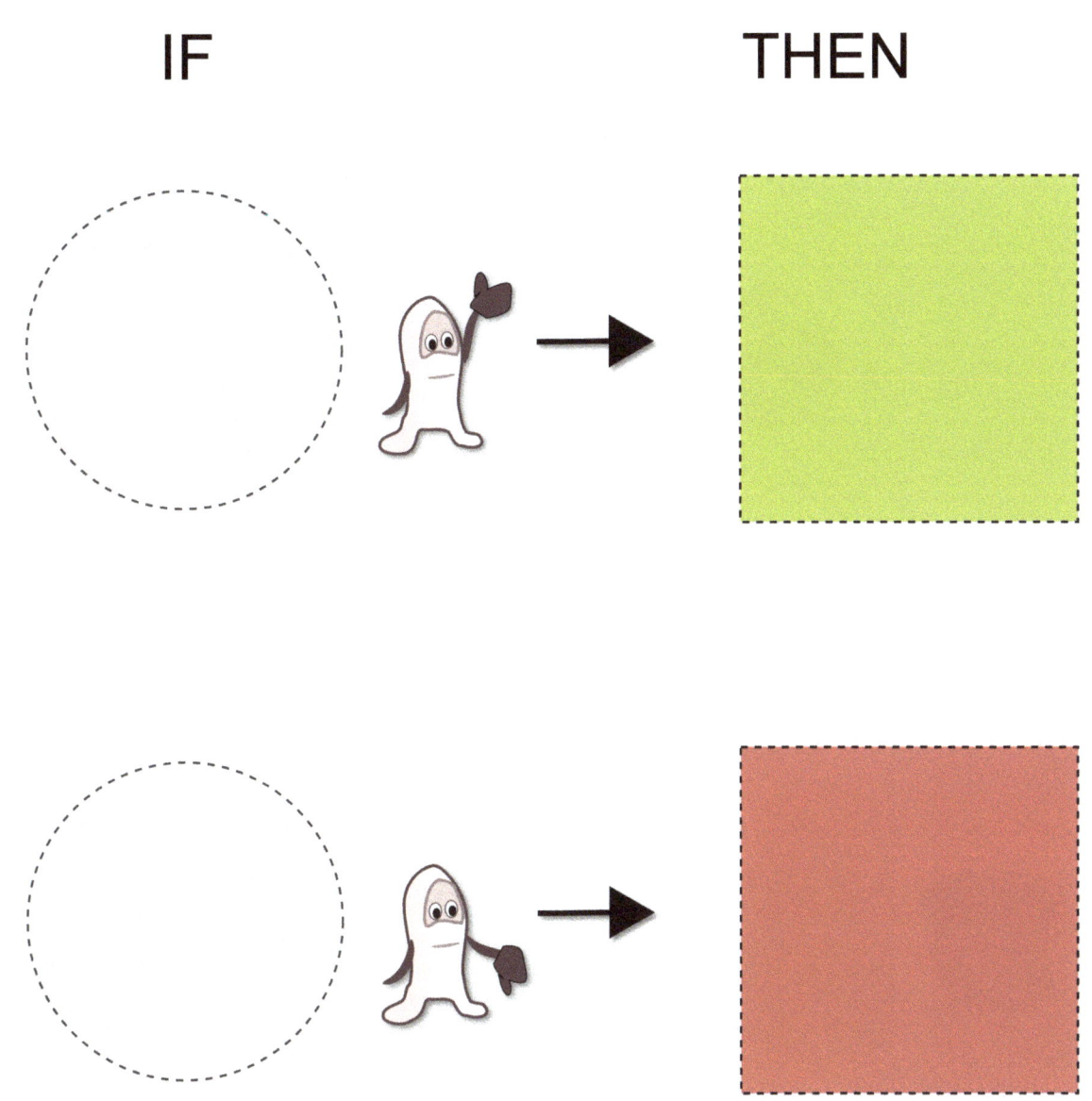

We ... use the oven ... measure sugar ... carry eggs ... mix eggs ... and bake the cookies. Give the circles a thumbs up or down! IF we do it, what happens THEN?

(Cut out the memory cards and play. Pair a circle with a square and place in the correct "IF" and "THEN" order.)

What toys do you like to play with?
The ball ... the iPad ...? Place a smiley on each toy.
(Use the big or small smileys on the next page.)

Cut out! Instructions on next page!

| 1 | 2 | 3 | 4 | / | // | /// | //// |

Instructions for the cut-outs on the previous page: The green circles should be placed on the three pages with the same images. They can also be used to limit the choices of toys in the last exercise. The numbers are an alternative to writing.

Want to practice more?

1) What does your child like (or not)? Which toys, colors, places, or fun things to do? Any favorite foods or drinks? Use the Smiley-cards in real life and stick them on fruits, toys, or pictures of things!

2) Tell your child why YOU like something.

3) Does your child know what friends and family members like? Do they like the same? How do we resolve it if two friends like the same toy or don't like to do the same things?

Bring Out — Mix — Shape Cookies — Eat

SMARTIES Bake & Like with Adrian and Super-A: Life Skills for Kids with Autism and ADHD
SMARTIES Workbook 1 © Jessica Jensen and Be My Rails Publishing 2021
All Rights Reserved. Please note, teachers may not copy workbooks for educational purposes.
It is not considered fair use if the copying provides replacements or substitues of workbooks.
The Adrian and Super-A Workbooks may be laminated and reused for the SAME student.
Pictograms kindly provided by www.sclera.be

Be My Rails Publishing
www.BeMyRails.com

Coconut Macaroons

The recipe equals 1dl sugar, 50g butter, 200g coconut, and 2 eggs.
12-15 minutes in 175°C.

tasting spoon

2 oz butter
0.5 cup sugar
2 eggs
8 oz / 2.5 cups shredded coconut

let the cookie batter swell for 10 min

20 cookies

350°
12-15 min

www.ingramcontent.com/pod-product-compliance
Lightning Source LLC
Chambersburg PA
CBHW041431040426
42444CB00022B/3497